What Love Can Do

Craig V. Taylor Jr.

Copyright © 2022 Craig V. Taylor, Jr.

All rights reserved. No part of this publication may be used or reproduced by any means, electronic, mechanical, graphic, including photocopying, recording, taping or by any information storage retrieval system or otherwise be copied for public or private use – other than "fair use" as brief quotations within articles and reviews – without prior written permission of the copyright owner.

ISBN: 978-1-954609-42-6

This book was printed in the United States of America

To order additional copies of this book contact:

LaBoo Publishing Enterprise, LLC
staff@laboopublishing.com
www.laboopublishing.com

Table of Contents

Introduction 1
The Beginning of Love 3
Love and Happiness 5
Morning Love. 6
Cooking Up Love 7
Love Driven 9
Good Love 11
Bad Love. 13
Self-Love 15
Love the Hate 17
Negative Love 19
Misguided Love. 23
Abusing Love 25
Safe Love 27
Forbidden Love 29
Powerful Love 31
Where Is the Love? 33
Toxic Love 35
Painting Explicit Love 37
Rekindled Love 39
For the Love of Music 41

Tattoo Love 43

Childish Love 45

Two Broken Love Stories 47

Married Love 49

Undisputed Love 51

Destined for Love 52

Fatherly Love 54

Godly Love 57

Timeless Love 59

True Love 61

Loving You 63

Love You to Death 65

Fake Love 67

Everything is Love. 69

Love is Life 71

Introduction

Love: it can be displayed in numerous ways. Some are good and some are bad, but at the end of the day, people categorize it as love. Whether it's towards a person, place, or thing, people's perception, or character, is what they perceived as love in their eyes. Throughout my time of living, I've been a witness to love on multiple scales. Through real life scenarios and storytelling, I will give you, the reader, the opportunity to see love from different angles that you may or may not know about when it comes to love. No one's love is the perfect love. With music being a big influence towards how I write, I included multiple artists and song titles throughout the book, dating from the 1970s through the early 2000s. Hopefully this gives you an opportunity to listen to these great hits I've grown to love while including them throughout the book, and how they were used. Enjoy.

The following song titles are mentioned within the book. Hopefully you manage to take the time to listen to them and enjoy them just as much as I have while making this book.

- Earth Wind & Fire – Devotion (1974)
- Earth Wind & Fire – Reasons (1975)
- Hall & Oates – Sara Smile (1975)
- Lenny Williams – 'Cause I Love You (1975)

- Queen – Somebody to Love (1976)
- Journey – Don't Stop Believin' (1981)
- Rick James & Teena Marie – Fire & Desire (1981)
- Evelyn King – Love Come Down (1982)
- Zapp & Roger – Computer Love (1985)
- Cameo – Candy (1986)
- Rick Astley – Never Gonna Give You Up (1987)
- New Edition – Can You Stand the Rain (1988)
- Haddaway – What is Love (1993)
- The Fugees & Lauryn Hill – Killing Me Softly (with His Song) (1996)
- Floetry – It's Getting Late (2002)
- Floetry – Say Yes (2002)
- TLC – Creep (2003)

The Beginning of Love

In the beginning of life, Love was present within us

Whether it was towards a person, place, or thing, Love's discovery was bound to reveal itself

The time and energy we put into the things we love defines some of the characters within us

As time allows us to live, grow, and experience, love begins to change

The things you once loved as a child won't be the same as you age into an adult

The amount of love you have as an adult will eventually change as you step into parenthood; if a child is something you choose to have

The love you have for yourself will someday want to extend itself in a form of partnership or marriage

So, self-love grows into a form of love to create unity or togetherness

It's a million-mile journey

Whether you walk it, ride it, drive it, bike it, or take flight, the trail will be waiting for you

The discoveries along the way will test you as a person

The ups and downs, the good and the bad

But when you take your final breath in the final restful state

Reflecting back at the million-mile journey, you'll begin to thank yourself for the journey of love you were able to take on

All because of love

It's worth every step

Love and Happiness

Happiness is inevitable

This world gives you everything it can to provide happiness

Love, does it give you a sense of happiness?

Does it provide comfort when you're in discomfort?

Is your happiness, for the love you express, in multiple things?

A person, place, or thing

Can it always be there when you need it?

Is there equal love for the things that you express happiness in?

Love and happiness

Hand in hand, their unity generates amazing wonders

No amount of money can buy something so priceless and free to all

Love and happiness, it feeds the soul to extend one's lifetime for a lifetime

So, the more you keep living, the more you should appreciate all things

The more it fulfills, the less hate and anger you'll endure

If everyone could feel this way, I'm sure the world, as a whole, could live in eternal peace

Morning Love

Daylight sun rays shining into my window, you're my morning love

A fresh new day of love like instant coffee

Rich nutrients to my heart like freshly squeezed orange juice

You give me all the support to make our love last

Laid up in bed, wrapped in each other's warm embrace

Allowing the alarm clock to keep reminding us to start our day

But we choose to keep snoozing so we can enjoy these cuddles for ten more minutes over and over

You are what defines a beautiful morning

Giving me your love to last all day

But giving me your time to last a lifetime

The fact you're so caring, I would never let a day end, or a sun set, knowing I didn't give the same affection that you've given me

We'll always rise and shine together

No matter the morning conditions, you make every morning a good morning

Cooking Up Love

A kitchen setting is where it all began

Where pantries and cabinets couldn't keep closed the impossible

Baking love in the kitchen, they never expected anything to come in a jiffy

Her love was sweet as cake, a birthday party per slice

His love was steel cut, and he wasn't serving any oats

He was more about keeping things continental, while she was more about big family feasts

But they mutually agreed on brunch, and that's when their spices began to form ingredients for a recipe

She had the juice to make him saucy

A love-like delight that caused her oven to bake

And as time became microwave fast, their love became a serving size for three

As problems brew and whistle like a tea kettle, the kitchen becomes hot

Love made them stay as they did what it took to cool things down

Devouring problems like a dish, they forked it still as they knifed it into edible pieces

And dessert was the aftermath for the accomplishments they finished in a spoonful

Now every guest, friend, and family member will step into their home with a delicious aroma coming from the kitchen

No matter the occasion, love has the ingredients to savor every flavor

Now everything about their love is finger-licking good

Bon Appetit

Love Driven

She loves to test my love

Whether I'm manual or automatic, she just doesn't know how much I'm driven by her love

She'll always be the finish line I'll race to

The way she sits on my lap and whispers what I like

Always turning me on, revving my engine loud

Roaring to her desires, she gets a feel of this horsepower

She never expects me to cruise when I'm in full throttle

Slowly exhausting like twin pipes, coming to the peak of our destination

Whether she puts it in reverse, or I jack her up, the peak will be our top priority

As my engine gases out, the drive I had is put in park

But just because the drive is gone, doesn't mean the race is over

In my best running shoes, I'll always chase for her love; even though I'm the only racer

I'm her first-place winner and she's my trophy

As I now whisper something in her ear to help lower her E brake

Trying to see if you're staying on the main streets or off road

So, what's your drive like?

I have the keys

Can I turn her on?

Because staying neutral isn't something we accelerate at

Good Love

I have that good love

It's not like everybody's love so you know it's only my love

Let my love someday fly you around the world

The timing may not be right, but I'm still love driven

Just allow me to open the door for you

Knowing I'm not rich, but I'm wealthy enough to show you we can fine dine

Elegant meals, dessert du jour, and have you whining for more wine

Telling me about your stressful day, even though you told me earlier your day was fine

But regardless, the plans I have will have you on cloud nine

As I run your bath and rub your feet, everything that was bothersome is now refined

Then dry you down, rub you in warm oils, and let this ice run down your spine

Let it wake you up like espresso, just to get you right

As I fill your ear with compliments that could last all night

Have you smiling and laughing as you cover your face because your cheeks blush so bright

As I compare myself to Superman as long as you're okay with being my kryptonite

Because your love makes me weak as we kiss and cuddle to sleep all night

As your favorite love song continues to repeat until the sun peaks to kiss the clouds in the daylight

COVID 19, my love for you is real pandemic

There'll never be enough distance between us to stop the love I have for you

No injection needed, I'll remain ill to the love and joy you quarantine me with

As long as the love I give is good, then everything is all good

Because I choose to live and breathe good love

Bad Love

Once upon a time, love was magnetized

Two opposites, but they made a connection

Through the ups and downs, they found a path to keep going

A blueprint for every trial, they were building good love

Good laughs, great passion

Date night weekends, bubbling over their love chemistry

The road seemed endless

But as smooth as the ride was, break downs and repairs became frequent

Finances were shuffled around

The ride drove differently, the tread started to wear

Love used to be the driver as it slowly transitioned to the passenger seat

And as other priorities started to become first place, love was soon trunk stuffed

All their history is about to be history, as their love becomes hair-line thin; waiting for anything to break it off

The dreams and goals are no longer the same

As nightmares are as real as the ones that happen in their sleep

Problems building, solutions unknown

As good laughs become tears of sadness

From dinner dates to isolation, love chemistry to block barriers

Their happily ever after seems so far away

I suppose this is why the best parts of their love was once upon a time

Wishing for fairy tail endings, it all ends in bad romance

Layers of unconditional love, trust, and communication has all been removed

Shedding the light on the remains of what only seems to be categorized as bad love

Self-Love

Everyday happiness is pursued and achieved

Putting myself above all, the only other people that would care is me, myself, and I

The world offers much stress and drama that rains repeatedly

Loving myself so, I've transformed my mind and body to become the windshield that allows the rain to hit and then roll off me

And as my body is massaged from head to toe, I begin to feel weightless as I transition to flotation therapy, and not sink from the world's weight

High on myself, learning there's more that I can offer myself that herbs couldn't journey me on

I'm more appreciative for all things life supplies me with

That I don't have to sponge up stress or feel pressured like a soda bottle after being shook

It's better to let go than to make myself feel restricted

To let things fall like September to remain hot when it's cold; and cold when it's hot

So, people can see I live everyday like a holiday

Oblivious to the chaos around me, I've managed to get a PhD in the study of me

Being both the teacher and the student, I schooled the principles within myself and graduated with high honors.

With love being my biggest cheerleader, I'm game for any situation

Because I know I don't need to be clutch when I'm winning from start to finish

Love the Hate

How did it get this far?

The friendly vibes, family on family

The chains that connected were at great links

The help and favors that were given

The random acts of kindness I displayed

Smiles and laughs together, how did you let it get this far?

From family-friend play to business matters, you changed up

As things needed to be compromised, you went from adult-like to being childish

As you're okay with wrecking a good foundation

Now that judgment and spite is mounted, I see now that you're the one that's damaged goods

Even in trash, you couldn't blend in

You was cool with me, now you hate me

Now I'm cool with you hating me

I love the aroma of it all

Because now I'm able to see your true colors when your character is no longer black and white

That you're happy with talking behind my back when I'm only a call or text message away

But the secrets you forget I know I've packaged and shipped with special delivery

I just hope you're not a fragile as you claim you aren't

Because the family you're wavy with, will be the same ones you'll cause to drift from you

So beyond forgiveness, I can't come to terms with you

Heart still beating, but you're dead to me; I only wish to lay you in your coffin

Because the hate you give, was what caused me to love to reap

I just hope you recapture your morals before I help them to rest in peace

Negative Love

Let's dive into a little love story

Where love, sex, and impatience are marked as scandal

Hidden love presents challenges, as couple gets shocking news

And they both have something that they couldn't deny

Now let's walk into the world of Bri

New home, working to have kids soon, happily engaged

With the wedding less than three months away, she often got excited when speaking about the ring exchange

Her fiancé worked long hours, but was very successful

Financially secure, whatever she wanted, he was able

Even told her to resign from being a swimming coach to be more focused on the upcoming wedding and planning for fertility

Because his swimmers weren't always so swimmingly

Her fiancé was everything she could ask for

But his testosterone wasn't the best, as she was always on pause for more

Often, he had trouble staying up, which often kept him down

More times than not, she pleasured herself to avoid it being a ghost town

But as her pleasure for more grew more and more, her patience began to shrink

Pleasuring herself to porn, it often made her think

Dominatrix, anal play, and BDSM; they often crawled into her mind

Thoughts became action as she discreetly looked for someone to give her this pleasure one good time

The discreet satisfaction she felt was plenty

But after time, one became many

With the fiancé working long hours, the wedding and fertility plans were starting to delay

She kept track of it all, but preferred to stick to child's play

Toys, vibrators, and beads

The toys used upon her allowed others to do whatever to fulfill her needs

But through it all there was only one guy that made her sex life feel alive

The chokes, the ropes, and shifting her legs around; a different type of drive

No protection in mind, but to only protect her wild life

Because if caught, she would no longer become a wife

Finally ending her double life, the wedding plans were back on track

She felt the urge to go back, but didn't draw back

Days after her encounter, she didn't feel right

The itching, the headaches, burning urination; so she decided to meet the doc for more insight

After further examination, she had herpes

Upon receiving the news, she dropped to her knees

Because now she was not sure if her fiancé would accept her for better or worse

For her sinful acts had left her with an incurable curse

So, months turned into days, as the wedding was near by

Hiding in makeup and both turning down sex on the fly

The day finally arrived to walk the aisle

Beautifully dressed in white, as she walked what seemed to be a long guilty mile

As she was about to confess her curse, he cut her off

Come to find out, what she had came from him all along

That sometimes he worked long hours and other times, he was "working" long hours

That those times he couldn't stay up, was because someone else already put it down

Even though he didn't know he had it until it was too late, this didn't excuse Bri from all her explicit dates

Both stood at the altar, and both walked away

Ringless and cursed, neither had nothing to say

Love makes us do strange things; and sometimes strange has no boundaries

Entertaining it has no positive rewards in the end

The negative love they had for one another gave them positive results

Results that, for now, don't have a resolvable answer

Misguided Love

TLC, I had a virgin mind when I found out you were a creep

The sandals and things you put in front of me, I was too young to put two and two together

Despite all the people you chose, I never questioned, "Why me?"

But my barrier was weakening as age grew upon me

Curiosity, women, male testosterone

And as my virginity cap was unsealed, you became the medicine that came in doses

Desires, temptation, sin

The guilt trips you took me on

To vacation on the islands of you

Giving me taste samples of the forbidden

As the night gets younger, you choose these moments to make me surrender

Wanting me to lose me for a worse version of me

It's getting late and all you want me to do is say yes, Floetry

After time, I loved it

It had me walking on the ceiling while looking on the floor

Discombobulated love as I couldn't separate what was actually love and what was you

But as arguments, drama, and disagreements came along from real love, you were over my shoulder to distract me and ease the pain

Allowing money to be bittersweet, the forbidden taste reoccurs as I dig myself free, only to dig my own grave

As maturity began to set in, I tolerated a lot from you

But I could see you were the problem I'd allowed to live on too long

As the love you gave me was nothing I could consider to be unconditional

Detaching myself from you, I often notice when you're attempting to come back

On the outside looking in, the welcome mat is where you'll stay as you continuously ring and knock at my door

Counseling myself to end this sincerely, I still have to start from the beginning

And figure out why you came and what I missed that caused you to come

And complete what hasn't been finished

So for now, I write to you

Dear Lust

Abusing Love

He moved a second state over to do right by his second marriage

The vibes from his hometown were never too far that the access wasn't accessible

The money he was getting from hard work, had him feeling untouchable

The hometown he wanted to escape, he actually carried with him

As the old love he divorced is reoccurring

The things he wanted often, made her uncomfortable

Hoping her third marriage was the charm, only to find more abuse

The multiple body marks clothed over

Chasing the money and attention came at the wrong price

The threesomes he inquired; they came, but she could never come

The career she left behind, she prayed to God she could manage to grab back as she leans away from the dirty money

Watching him do more lines of crack than windshields

If he was in a drug filled stadium, he'll be nosebleed high

And whenever he stresses, the angel dust brought him closer to heaven

As much as their love has been up and down, they are bound to one another

Stacking life's problems like pancakes, the syrup they wish they had to sweeten things wasn't doctor prescribed as it kept them sedated

As she applies pressure to her hands and knees, praying to God, her faith is working overtime

To bypass the pain and challenges that come from the aftermath of his usage and her abuse

Hoping her soul still has a fighting chance to change them around

But after dealing for so long, can she will herself to leave if the love no longer exists within herself?

Despite knowing he'll die if she goes, she prays herself to sleep

Only to wake up daily still trying to find the answers for her prayers that are still pending

Safe Love

With my love you don't have to worry about your heart thinking while your brain is in love

I'm not trying to pose any danger, so this love I'm guaranteeing you is caution free

Prison confinement, maximum security

This love received cannot escape

No visitors needed to try to riot my secured love

Safe, happy, and content

Never expecting you to tear or water in sadness, even if your allergies were bad

Hugging you and kisses galore, trying to push me away; my arms are locked around you

The little things you never received will catch you by surprise daily

The good morning calls, the "just because" gifts

The flowers and hand holding everywhere we go

Locking in everything your love gives me, amnesia pops up fast for the key I never kept up with

But never forgetting to pop up with my presence every time I pop in your mind

I want your love to be safe and secure; like keep your money in the bank safe, love

As the bills pile up, we can vacation whenever knowing we don't have to come home to a single bill piled up

Deposit me your love and you'll get it back with interest

Never have to take out a loan when you're secure, so them loan calls can leave you alone

And if they don't, then they can pay you for your time

Because your time towards others, without me, is expensive

Your presence is my daily present

I'm trying to be good to you, but don't call me a good boy

I'm not here to fetch or give you a bone

I'm proving that not all guys are dogs

Because all the dogs you normally talk about aren't guaranteed to go to heaven

I'm giving you daily peace now, so this heaven I'm given can match what's expected when you do reach heaven

Forbidden Love

He wakes up hungover in a bed that's not his own

With a woman that claims she's single like he is

But even without her ring on, he still sees her ring print while she's peacefully sleeping

It all happened so fast, like a cool quick breeze during a heatwave

From work, to the bar, she locks eyes on him

Even if he wanted to be quarantine discreet, she'll be able to detect him; even with his mask on

She flirts with him to generate a vibe to his timid style

But as the ice from his drink sinks, glass after glass, his impressions changed while she sweet talked him awhile

Now he's ready to think and say what he feels about her in graphic quotes

Karaoke lip syncing each other to "Sara Smile" by Hall & Oates

Seeing if this transitions to the bedroom, but she was already grabbing her car keys so they can leave

To give him a special treatment in bare that her husband could never get her to achieve

After a while, they were like Rick James; she provided the fire that sparked his desire

Music loud, phones silenced

She moans and groans that he's the best, man

He swipes her ring off just to hold her hand

The kisses, the lip biting

The gripping, the holding

Lasting all night, they slept most of the day away

Back to his timid form, he knows things will never be the same

As much as they enjoyed each other's company

Because if her husband finds out, they'll no longer be best friends

Because while he's another state over, tending to an ill family member, his wife was giving something to the best man that'll be bittersweet to remember

Powerful Love

Da-da, daddy, dad

I've watched them both grow from infants to toddlers

From crawling, to walking, and holding my hand to take me places

And I even have to run, since they think everything is race worthy

The loving care from their mom, the daredevil playfulness of me, the love from this family grows more and more

That we all will love, but when things get serious, and lessons are to be taught

It doesn't mean we don't love them any less

It's to prepare them for life's long journey ahead that isn't so playful

That whatever partners they are bound to cross, will have to fight to match the love the family gives them before categorizing themselves as real partners in my eyes

These kids are the blood in my body and heart that forever pumps, that keeps me going

That I'll forever be in their corner, and never back them into one

Growing older by the day, the joy they enlighten the atmosphere with keeps me young

So, I can stay a superhero in their eyes for decades to come

They are what makes me feel powerful when the world, on the outside, looks towards money and riches

Mother and father

Daughter and son

A family that loves together, stays protected together

That's as powerful as it comes

Where Is the Love?

Where is the love?

He probably thinks this often, but never says

A father that's done a lifetime of things, but doesn't share a life with him

Birthdays and Christmas are the only times they seem to share life

As my mind boils in frustration for the things that don't seem fair

Because the father figure he wants to adore, will only give him two days out of a year and nothing more

But to me, you're a 365-winter season, you're cold to him on a yearly basis

So many times I've tried to figure out why

Because he's not what you "expected", so you feel like a failure in your eyes

And choose to keep a sun visor present when he comes across your presence like a bright day

He's a puzzle piece in which you refuse to piece together

The picture-perfect lifestyle you enjoy, won't allow you to see the bigger picture

The pride and ego will haunt you for the times you'll wish you could have had with him when you finally lay to rest

And even when he has options of fun things to do, he'll still choose you; as you choose other options

If you ever read this and it brings you shame, then I'm applying pressure

You have the health and the wealth, you need to do better

Because the love you display him is a 2 rating on a scale of 10

Where is the love?

I've tried to identify it with a magnifying glass, but still couldn't spot it

Toxic Love

What is love?

If she could summarize her love to an artist, she Haddaway

To be married in the years of once upon a time

To now finding herself in the thick of leaving, but wanting to stay

What is love?

Years beyond the puppy love stage, she fights to save her marriage

Despite her being in the wrong and admitting to her own dirt

She still gave him a child and seeks to lean her faith towards God

But the trust seal could never reattach as pettiness brewed

Arguments raised, emotions are challenged

To the point where words become physical, and body markings became present

If he was a ball player, then his aggression for her came after the fourth quarter

In overtime, he's an abusive playmaker to her

Just check the scoreboard

Beats her mentally and physically to remain undefeated

The scores are tallied up on the amount of times she's bled by his hands and cried from his words

The highlights show it all, a real abusive MVP

Separation within the marriage, she uses her loneliness to tap into selfcare to heal

As he's off to pursue a partner of his own, he still finds love and comfort from the one he vowed to

She too pondered to accelerate some fantasies, but stays committed to him

As damaged as they both are, the years and time they've amounted together couldn't allow them to move on from one another

Both coming and going, but never as one, the revolving door could never stay closed

Looking for answers and clarity that's been miscommunicated, this cliffhanger is inching over the edge

In the end, the children unaccounted for, will pay the ultimate price for the things they were never able to resolve

As we begin to see more and more why the children of this present time are more and more dysfunctional

Painting Explicit Love

After a night of dance and drinking, their lovely date is about to end explicit

For he knows she's submissive as the clothes she had became dismissive

She looks at him and sees heaven in his eyes

As he lays her down, he raises hell as she brings the demon out the man

To the point where the sky shines a golden glow as Satan applauds and says amen

Even though they were housed, she enjoys touring his city

But she loves to go downtown

Deep in his Manhattan, she blows like Chicago

Her legs were like tracks, she just waiting on his train to arrive

As fast as the fastest train, his arrival might be sooner than expected

A basket of fruit is what she tastes like

Body shaped and firm like a pear, but a peachy personality

Unpeeling his peelings to reveal his banana was to her appealing

Kissing on her candy apple bottom, licking on her cherry top

Tasting her fruit punch juices, he received a pitcher full

Pouring out, his cup shaped mouth is ready with ice

Spilling all over the floor, he's trying to cork it, but her wet Kegels has him slipping out from what he couldn't see; like black ice

Like a painter, he's an artist stroking a masterpiece

She's far from a blank canvas, but he's expressing ideas and creations

Painting her insides like a wall of art, "The Scream" was the painting she reacted like

Love painting the perfect picture, no debit card or amount of cash can buy it

Let the buyers wave their checks for this explicit painting that they want to study more

But love voided all the offers because it has already checked out

Rekindled Love

A junior high fling that never managed to become high school sweethearts, she figured he was cute without the E

No bloodshed, but as time caused them to take separate paths, their detour caused them to merge again

Getting inquiry on his story, she schooled him a textbook of past memories that was more revolutionary than history class

Matching the vibes and energy, they agreed to meet

A date full of laughs and small talk

Extending from noon to evening, they settled in with a dinner and some movies

The feelings were visible just by the way they talked, so the cuddles weren't a blind surprise

Holding each other close, claustrophobic would have been claustrophobic

As clothes that divided them was removed so skin can touch

Like refurbishing old love to a kindle, they rebooted old into new love as she roll-called his name over and over

Living and loving the moment, the past is still future relevant

As the relationship they wish to have will create problems they'll separate their merged road

In the words of Evelyn King, their love had to come down

Reality was more prominent than their dream that they'd wish to never wake up from

So as much as the rekindled flame of years past in modern time was able to light, it wasn't worthy of burning on for years to come

Only to assume all flames flame out eventually

For the Love of Music

If my poetry was on the operating table, music would be the doctor

Open heart surgery, pour the love in so it can be put back on beat

Let the notes, beats, and lyrics pump into those veins

So, when the heart starts to pump and thump, the brain will begin to jump when it was at a stump

Music, an emotional and lyrical dictionary

I read you time after time

To match you with my reality, to birth my own art

A father to so much poetry, it never crossed my mind to vasect after crossing 300

If music is their mom, their existence will live beyond my lifetime

Eyes flooded with pages of work, as music leaks out my ears, my brain feels like sex on the beach; but my pullout couldn't leave the beach

So, as I continue to write on, I expect music to be the WD-40 to prevent me from starting to rust

When the world knows how to drive me crazy, you become the mood stabilizer to keep me sane

Spreading your love to the lives of many, but still never too far away from me; you regulate on a global scale

Trying to find a mood that doesn't match you is damn near impossible

Even when I have days I feel powerless, you pour over me like rain that forever reigns

And find ways to dissect and redefine me to every detail

For every goal I crossed, you've helped make every one of them obtainable

Tattoo Love

My body is a work of art

Clean, muscular, naked

The brands I choose to ink on me are a representation of me, and the things I love

The things my mind creates, I'll place them on me

To endure the pain, for the art I love

Sitting in the chair, hearing the needle buzz

Adrenaline bleeding out, just to masterpiece my masterpiece

Love is pain

The love I desire often hurts

But the aftermath is an artistic beautiful scar

As one becomes many, the joy slowly turns into an addiction

I could go cold turkey for years, and it'll take only one hit to reactivate those cravings

Chest covered, sleeved without fabric

Yes, my body may be naked, but I'm covered

All for the love of art

May my blood someday bleed ink, so my addiction and soul can feel sanctified

That my new body will forever be covered by heavenly creations

And that this love I've manifested, through ink, can be shared with the world

Childish Love

A shy kid, new to love, he sees the one he admires

He sees her, but as she passes him, he loses his tongue

His quietness said it all

Her gentle smile and settling eyes passed him by, just like his chance

Like candy in a classroom, he wants her all to himself

No time for phone games, but he wasn't sure how many moves he had left on his candy crush

Time after time, he lost repeatedly

At the playground:

Hanging for a chance at the monkey bars; another chance slides away down the slide

Hide and seek:

He manages to find everybody, but hides when finding the one he wants most

Spin the bottle:

Those seven minutes in heaven were normally spent alone when the bottle lands on nobody

Out of frustration, he stands up to himself, but folds over as she approaches him once again

But she gives him her number with a heart drawn over the folded note

After all the shots missed, she was the one that referee her way for him to score

Young puppy love

Cute and innocent, the older crowd doesn't expect it to last long

As they bond, grow, and laugh, they slowly learn one another more

Trying to see who hangs up first; testing to see who's more loyal to who

The gentle clinginess and hand holding is how they define liking one another

In fear of germs and cooties that come from kissing, they hug consistently

The cute nicknames and after school strolls is how they define their partnership

Thinking what they have will last a lifetime

When their lives have yet to truly unfold

Two Broken Love Stories

She's been broken-hearted too many times

He's been fed up with being lonely for so long

She's forgiven him time after time

He's seeking something more serious after multiple failed relationships

She's so scared to be lonely, but she can still see his potential

Whenever he tries to date, it never ends well

She prays that things will change, but will it heal her?

He's dated many thinking forever can come from a first date

She ponders if she's the answer to her own prayer

He's been turned down so many times, that sadness spirals into depression

She packs enough that he wouldn't notice

He ponders suicide alone until his child crawls to his direction

She leaves her broken love to repair her heart

His child, still learning to talk, says enough to silence his thoughts

She wipes those final tears, and begins to pursue what makes her happy

He pours the love into his son to make him a great man someday

She's learning to love herself more, so she can heal from the wounds of her broken love

He gives life lessons to his son, so when manhood comes, he'll try to avoid the things that will cause him to have broken love

Married Love

For better or for worse, right?

We said "I do"

But those things don't come to mind as the years begin to stack

When the kids come into play and small arguments combine into something big

The disconnects and the petty disagreements, as problems weigh on us

And somehow the only time our communication is up to par, is when intimacy is involved

It was unhealthy for sure, but we said I do

Having to distance myself from that, I had to remember why I chose you

The laughs, the dates, the life you give me that others don't

The joy we have is irreplaceable

The time we put into one another, the timeless acts of affection we never accounted for

The love we bridged together, we crossed together

We both did wrong that caused our unity to become puzzle pieces

But through it all, we're still here

To fix us, to repair our love

God is knocking at the front door, it's time to invite him in

Because through all the cycled problems and chaos, I still love you

And through Christ, nothing can pressure us

I wouldn't want no one else to side with but you

I said I do, and so did you

So, let's continue to do this

And do it together

Undisputed Love

In a world full of straight roads, there are just as many that curve off

That there are roads that are meant to turn or even curl

Not everyone's way can be the right way; but judgment often tries to cause certain roads to be dead ends

So many mile markers you've driven by, so many signs that may've passed you by

Doesn't mean you can't turn back and they'll be gone forever

Some of those signs you'll come to meet again

Such as love

It's okay to love who you love

Even if they carry the same parts as you

The same path you think you're walking alone, you'll find many others on

It's better to be visible than camouflage these personalities that people would rather see invisible

Love who you love, because nothing is guaranteed

That dead-end road may end up being a bridge to endless possibilities

With love, may you forever live young, wild, and free

Destined for Love

She has a family to love; a fatherless one for a while

The time she took to care for her ill and abusive mom, along with a younger sibling, it clouded her judgment on love

She simply wanted to be a queen to somebody to love, but ended up settling for less on a few occasions

Expecting better from an already bad relationship, she sacrificed often to keep them pleased

Items, favors, and sex

Referenced like a tool, she was used often

The weight of her family and relationships stressed her daily

To seek true peace and happiness seemed invisible to the naked eye

Emotionally wrecked from peer pressure, rape, and being bullied, her life felt unfair

The anchored down problems, and flaws of her own, will drown her; never to gasp air for real love

Until a new gentleman comes along that she discovers

He gave her smiles and joy often

Gave her bravery and fearless judgment to boost her confidence

Valued her time as it refilled her soul

And just when she was ready to gift him her love, her previous relationship gift wrapped it in chlamydia

Unaware of the setback, she thought this would cause him to leave her isolated and alone

But it was the complete opposite

That her anchor was lifted as air was drawn

The cracks and chips to her heart were repaired

As time and years build their relationship, vows and children soon came afterward

As new challenges come and go, they'll do what's best and necessary to keep their love pure

To avoid the anchor of years past

Fatherly Love

A father figure still pursuing figures

But the family I've made puts my imaginary mind in the millions

Creating endless memories no price tag item can replace

This love is mastered without a MasterCard, so this family I amount is priceless

Brought them a house to solidify our lives

But my princess sees this as a castle in her eyes

As my prince is a peek-a-boo master of disguise

The hugs, kisses, tears, and boo-boos that come my way

The bedtime stories and fighting the monsters under the bed on the daily

Kiss them before work, so this align of work doesn't feel like labor

Being their guide through their lives are the moments I savor

Far from perfect, but they see perfection

A hero with no weakness, a teacher with out-of-the-box lessons

At times I'm learning from them as they get more and more verbal

360, one of each, with their mom and I; this completes my full circle

They give me tears, I provide comfort

They give me sadness, I provide laughter

Giving them the world, but more pros than cons, so they can always laugh harder than prerecords for sitcoms

Knowing the word, but they'll never be a victim of suffering

For the things that cause questions of their future, I'll be accessible for every answer

They give me love, I give them fatherly love

Keeping them lifted mentally and physically, I pray that they go higher than the skies above

Idolize these credentials because deadbeats have me outclassed

As some women, and the internet, try to categorize good dads and deadbeats as the same flock

But I'll be the owl in the night preying to feed my nest while looking back like who?

Because I can see the lies from a bird's eye view

Like a totem pole, I sit below to hold the family to its highest regards

Holding them together like elastic, while many assumed I'll pop like rubber bands

The daddy chants keep me fueled for the many journeys ahead

Because the only time I'll stop is when pi ends

Hopefully my math adds up to the amount of love I won't subtract

Godly Love

When power seems untamable, I turn to you

Each second of breath I breathe, is a blessing worth praising

When the world sees an ocean view, I'm more observant of the rivers of where our blessings flow

Father, father, father

I stretch my hands to thee

God almighty, you are almighty

The love I have for you can be told until my final day of rest

You are what liberates us all when the world is finally unshackled and able to see the sin once the blindfold is removed

Satan always trying to box you in, but you know how to create your own angles

Everyday you're testing me

To make me a stronger me

To challenge my faith when trials don't seem fair

To see if my religion is tempted to do temptation

I love you and thank you for the pieces in place in my life to help me walk in the light

The faithlessness you have for me is miraculous

The sins cast around me, you still give me a path that sometimes isn't always visible

I love you and thank you for the things I've been given, for the unknown ahead of me, and the things I've taken for granted

The lessons received, I take to heart

The joy you bring me is irreplaceable

The love you gave me, I try to share with others

Because all love is God's love

Timeless Love

You'll never have to time my love for you like clockwork

I'd rather give you a faceless watch so you can try to time how often my love is predictable

How you once counted every second, now I'm trying to make every second count for the love I have for you

Year after year, season after season

Everything around us is changing, but our love remains the same

The timeframes that passed us will forever be rememberable as our love evolves more and more

Turning good into great, we can laugh at our previous relationships

How it often felt like punching a time clock, when we preferred 24-hour shifts

But as temporary as they were, this is forever

As the next generation ahead view this history

How love was done the right way for centuries that decades couldn't catch up to

Time me if you want, I'm forever

When love is spoken, my life and body of work will be mentioned

I'll make sure Time will be presented to vouch for me

Beginning, middle, and end

From start to finish, I poured out love that never drained me

Because this love has been endless that time has managed to capture

True Love

The love I've given is a true blessing

Heaven on earth type of love, I'm as almighty as it comes

Loving you has always been so real

No amount of sleep can dream up something this good

To laugh while we're young as we grow old together

This type of love that's out of this world

Burning and shining like the sun

With so much beauty blinding me, I often find it hard to walk and balance myself on these stars so that space doesn't keep us far apart

Let the world film our love like a movie

We'll make sure the viewers get their popcorn worth

That we have the action, drama, comedy, and suspense; but I still catch myself waking up knowing I'm still dreaming when I see a superstar daily

To have you and to hold everyday

To be that reminder that if you're running out of love, to simply run to me

I'll slow you down so you can read all my signs of love that you won't miss

So, you know I'm here for all the sunny weather love; and I'll be here like New Edition when you think I can't stand in the rain

Through the earth, wind, and fire, I'm devoted to you if you needed any reasons

And if you ever thought I planned on giving up on you, ask Rick Astley what you mean to me

You're forever mine, you're my world

You're worth protecting, you're my favorite

Cameo all the different flavors of you, and the original you still would be my favorite piece of candy

True love has many, many chapters within the book of love

I just want to make sure our love is worth reading cover to cover

Loving You

I didn't need Computer Love to search for you

My body has been present for all this loving

My soul attached to yours as I slipped on your ring

As young as I was, I wanted to prove that I'm worth it all

That the two of us can start our own team

Protection guaranteed, prayer daily

That if one of us fall short, that the other is always available

To have more laughable tears than sad ones

Perfection is never perfect, but this marriage will aim to stay on course

I need you

Always thinking you're bothering me, only means to me that I'll never be alone

Through sickness and health, like we vowed

These babies, this home, our life together; no one could ever replace

This love will forever be the ice that runs down my back that gives me chills

So, the things I do, I do them for you and the family

To protect, to provide

To be the husband you dreamt many nights about

To be the dad you and I both wanted for them

You're my strength when the world starts to make me fatigue

When many see our flaws and try to use it to create damage between you and I

Attempting to create tension and arguments between you and I

We'll humble the hate to filter out love

The journey is worth it, so don't stop believing

But just in case you have any doubt or questions, you're free to ask

My answer will remain the same

It's because I love you

Lenny Williams sung it best

Love You to Death

Like a ghost in a movie, your love haunts me like no other

Instead of scaring me into a heart attack, I'd rather donate my heart to you

So, you know my love for you only beats for you

Because I love you to death

Risked my love for you daily because I knew one day it would eventually be gone

Because I remember those times your emotions were hanging out the window

Either expecting me to be the cliffhanger to save you, or dangling in suspense, you were careless from a lack of true love never received

As I gave you time, time after time

The love in you returned that didn't stay away

Reuniting your love, while draining mine, I loved it though

Giving you all that I had meant that I would be the best you'll ever have

Trips out the state, mini vacations galore

Gifts that sparked your eyes, flowers every payday

Day after day, I showed you heavenly pampering, while I was sizzling on Hell's barbeque

A better world you can envision, as mine slowly began to burn, but I loved it

Through it all, your happiness and blissful love is all I wanted you to endure

Even if it meant losing all of mine

The love I have for you is worth dying to protect, just to see you smile often while killing me softly

Giving you my love is the death penalty I am willing to take

Sacrificing me for a better you, it's no mystery behind it, just selfless love

What can I say?

I've retooled your love and given you my own

Never again shall you know how it feels to be without, as I now embark on this journey, I once saw you on

Lifeless as I become, I've loved knowing I've loved you 'til the very end

Fake Love

My love can restore some salvaged lives

My presence can ease their minds

Trying to be more grateful in all things, but the many around me remain gratefully ungrateful

Granted, they never had a reason to point a gun at me, I can see the killer instincts in their eyes

Keeping them in close proximity, the enemies love to reap on my forgiving love

To smile in my face as they half ass clean the damage they've caused

Waiting for the opportunity to prey and taint my love and attempt to cheer me up; only to make "I told you so" statements

Never knowing the difference in being wrong and doing wrong, they claim they're doing things out of love

But how wrong is this distributed love if they never had the right love themselves?

Treating love like a coat hook and hanging it up

Ripping the phone cord out of the wall, and still expecting love to be connected like a speed dial call

Sending prayers up for being a lefty, because none of this is alright

But I'll mirror the smiles they show me, knowing our perceptions on love is disconnected and permanently cut

Moving forward, my moves will be visible like white ink on white paper

To see if they can feel me like braille, even though this isn't a read along

Blindly trying to talk and communicate with me

Trying to converse, but not really saying nothing

So, what is the meaning behind their words when I know the love is fake?

Everything is Love

Everything is love, everything was love

A fairly young couple in puppy love

Saw it in each other's eyes they wanted forever love

That fun love, that good love, that made everything all love

Claimed it in their vows, so their love become our love

As they began a new path of unconditional love

The love was strong the love was right, that they ended up making love

Small challenges and trials came and went to divide their love

But all failed; they had strong love

But too many times his love wasn't her love

That the challenges of life that was passable, passed into self-love

Which made unconditional love into weak love

Seeking on sin, the love he found was the wrong love

The trill of sinful love made him abandon real love

Caught in the act, he gets no love

Drama is an all-time high, as he battles for family love

Thinking in her head, how could you hurt love?

But through all the pain, there is still love

As they seek holy love to rebuild love

So, everything can be back at happy love

Because as much hurt as the world offers, they are thankful for love

Everything is love, everything is love

Unity in love is always the right love

Love is Life

Love is love

When needed, it shall provide

Good or bad, it will be there

The journey is often unexpected

The path is sometimes blinding

You alone are the guide for yourself to make love worth striving

Life is a daily test

Testing your character, testing your well-being

To see what's destined for you once you've crossed paths to love

Will it be everything you expect it to be?

Will it be everything you destined for it to be?

Love is unmatched because no love is the same

As is life

Make the best of the moments that come your way

Invite the flaws and challenges that love gives, it is a test after all

Just make sure you pass

So, when you've finally conquered them all, you'll start to succeed in all things

Life and love, yin and yang

One can't exist without the other

Perfect balance

What good is life with nothing to love?

So love what you can

Because life is the best love you can have

www.ingramcontent.com/pod-product-compliance
Lightning Source LLC
Chambersburg PA
CBHW051704090426
42736CB00013B/2540